A Brief Guide to Objective Inquiry

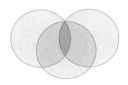

Jerry Pattengale

TRIANGLE PUBLISHING

A Brief Guide to Objective Inquiry
Jerry Pattengale

Direct correspondence and permission requests to one of the following:

E-mail: info@trianglepublishing.com
Web site: www.trianglepublishing.com
Mail: Triangle Publishing
1900 W. 50th Street
Marion, Indiana 46953
USA

Pattengale, Jerry
A Brief Guide to Objective Inquiry

Graphic design: Lyn Rayn
Photography: Kevin Welch
(unless otherwise noted)

ISBN-13: 978-1-931283-20-5
ISBN-10: 1-931283-20-6

Printed in the United States of America

Dedication

To Johnny Taylor, 1928-2005

A Brief Guide to Objective Inquiry was written at our little farm between Fairmount and Marion, in the historic black community of Weaver, Indiana. Does my neighborhood's history bias me? Yes, if by bias one means a predisposition to view something or someone in a certain way. Where a predisposition becomes a fault is when new or enlarged data calls for a modification in one's perception, but one refuses to acknowledge the new truth. Living in Weaver influences some of the questions I ask, sensitizes me to various issues, and it certainly helps to interpret some of the answers I uncover. Does it mean that my work is less objective than others? No, not in and of itself. To hold opinions based on limited or imperfect knowledge is to be a finite human. This very dedication is an example of having biases inform the choice of honoree, yet also committing to be objective in the face of new information.

This book is dedicated to Johnny Taylor, one of the last two descendants of the original Weaver family. The recorded and informal history of this community allows anyone, not just friends, to conclude objectively that he lived a fulfilling life and contributed significantly to his town, county and country. He was a patriot, a veteran, and father of veterans. In a touching ceremony his eldest son removed the highest medal for bravery from his uniform and placed it on his father shortly before the casket was closed. Johnny is "buried" at the Weaver cemetery in a mausoleum atop 2,200 African American graves—all on a half-acre plot.

Is this difficult to believe—so many graves on such a little stamp of land? How can you determine if my words are true? Or if Johnny Taylor lived at all, let alone was a patriot and local hero?

First, you might turn to Appendix One and read "An Afro at the Crossroads." This is a reprint of an article about Weaver and a glimpse into utilizing objective inquiry in our daily lives—to find intersections between our new knowledge and our routines, to find meaning. The article is an artifact, a piece of information that helps to corroborate the larger story of Johnny's life.

And should you dig very deeply in the Weaver cemetery, you'll discover that Johnny and his ancestors have a rich history, and that Johnny committed his life to a noble cause—the protection and promotion of human dignity. He also believed that the human story reflects both the need for God and the power of divine love. While our objective inquiry may not prove a supernatural intervention in human affairs, as Johnny taught, it can show that such intervention is the most logical explanation for such things. Is this my bias showing through or is this an objective conclusion based on the best information available? I believe that the latter has informed the former.

Jerry Pattengale
January 2, 2007

Contents

Introduction

Why the pursuit of objectivity?

Objective inquiry may be impossible in its purest form, but its pursuit is necessary. The quest for knowledge is quintessentially human, and the recognition that biases exist is essential to this journey. We should utilize the best information at hand to make the best possible conclusions. In short, we want to know the truth. Whether Christian or pagan, politically liberal or conservative, and regardless of our ethnic and cultural profiles, we bring different perspectives to the search for truth. Objective inquiry should be common ground for scholars of all stripes, minimizing biases and, where possible, neutralizing them.

The thesis of this little book is that the corroboration of reliable sources is essential for meaningful dialogue about the past. This text represents the key aspects of this foundational process of objective research. It also places the growing need for objective inquiry amidst today's philosophical and cultural trends. While the interpretation of evidence requires a second step of forming and supporting hypotheses, as noted in Appendix Four, objective inquiry begins with identifying the best sources of evidence and where that evidence is the most certain—where more than one source sheds light on the same thing.

The term "objective inquiry" implies being impartial and not being subjective. Objective knowledge is usually associated with the scientific and historical methods of research. Conversely, we associate subjective inquiry and knowledge with opinions. While opinions might indeed coincide with the conclusions from objective inquiry, they usually lack credibility beyond the scope of relationships and spheres of influence.

Through objective inquiry we show due diligence to the rules of research that are public—objective inquiry welcomes objective critique. Objectivity takes seriously relevant evidence and does not reject or falsify it when it seems to contradict our personal beliefs or opinions.

Sensible approaches to objective inquiry exist and help us to stand on common ground as learners—whether seasoned scholars or first-year collegians. We may disagree on the interpretation of data or new knowledge, but we should be able to ascertain the foundational facts in a mutually respected and acceptable manner.[1]

"Critical thinking skills" surface in almost every university's list of desired outcomes for its graduates—and this implies that critical inquiry skills are not only possible but measurable. There is widespread agreement that any college graduate should be able to think critically. This does not imply that a graduate has become a sage, but it rather intimates that brilliance and wisdom are dependent on reasonable analytical skills. Objective inquiry is a manifestation of these skills.[2]

The following text is an adaptation of the first chapter in *The History of World Civilizations from a Christian Perspective.* The content below has already been used with a variety of college courses because of its interdisciplinary application.

The presence of this Roman mile marker in Capernaum is one of many artifacts corroborating the biblical account of Roman occupation of Israel. These markers are cited in writings from the Early Church and in the journals of numerous pilgrims to the Holy Land. The collective evidence points to a "0" marker within Jerusalem. See David Livingston, "Locating Biblical Bethel Correctly—Part II," *Ancient Days* (web version), 2003.

While it highlights history among the social sciences, its principles and observations apply to any field of study. The historical examples are included to provide a context or big picture on which to hang our discussions. As I note in *The Motivated Student,* "The Big Picture Approach" resonates with the way we approach life, and the way we experience it. Likewise, the following historical examples provide discussion points that will help to unpack these principles.[3]

The Dead Sea Scrolls were found in the caves at Qumran; believed to be associated with the Essenes until the Romans ended their occupation in A.D. 68. Pictured above is Cave 4, where 122 scrolls or scroll fragments were found.

While I have biases, I am cognizant of the need to exercise objective inquiry. To label someone as "biased" has a derogatory connotation today, implying a disregard for objectivity. And, many people do approach studies in such a manner. However, the truth is that while we all have biases, most scholars subject themselves to commonly accepted research methods. Biases linger, but rational processes rule.

I am a Christian in the educational profession with degrees in history, religion, and psychology—from both private and public universities. You might ascertain that I'm likely to be biased via my educational path, but concomitantly these reputable schools have helped me to learn sound research processes. In this *Google* age, you can come to a reasonable conclusion by tracking my professional record. In doing so, you might also catch my vocational focus. My passion is to utilize my education in assisting readers to understand their life purpose, not merely to facilitate the transmission of knowledge.[4]

Through objective studies of historical movements and leaders we can begin to understand the nature of causes—some are noble and others ignoble. Many causes are in between, and some are even neutral. Through an objective inquiry process I continually arrive at conclusions that not only provide a fuller sense of reality, but that reaffirm the benefit of values consistent with biblical injunctions. I am not letting my religious beliefs determine my conclusions, but admittedly I allow such beliefs to help me to understand more clearly their meaning.

This first-century Jewish tomb (also called "Herod's Tomb") corroborates the use of tombs with large rolling stones mentioned in the New Testament account of Christ's resurrection from the dead (Matthew 27:60; Mark 15:46; Luke 23:53; John 20:1). Historians often advocate a "three-source rule," that is, looking for at least three independent sources for verification of a fact. Other first-century tombs exist, and each of the above New Testament records represents a separate ancient source, each with extant manuscripts within a few decades of the event. The appendices of the Nestle-Aland *Greek New Testament* include detailed charts that identify the earliest copies supporting these passages and their locations (usually in a museum or library). The inscription bearing the name of Pontius Pilate is also shown—another artifact that supports the narrative leading to the tomb event described in the above passages.

Gaining a Historical Perspective:

History and Truth

When we read about important events, how do we know they are true? In 1517, did Martin Luther really nail his "95 Theses" to the Wittenberg door? In 1963, did Martin Luther King, Jr. actually write "Letter from Birmingham Jail" from the Birmingham jail? And how do we know with certainty that Jesus lived in Galilee and died in Jerusalem in the first century? Are these stories fact or fiction?

Numerous *primary sources* attest to the *truthfulness* of the above events. The stories are indeed factual, and historians are reasonably sure of their key components. Though we don't know most historical accounts exhaustively, we can know their essence accurately.

For example, we may not know the wood type of the Wittenberg door or the names of those who watched Martin Luther nail up his list of ninety-five discussion topics. However, we do know of his basic actions around that time—his struggles with church doctrine, his professorship in Wittenberg, the existence of a Catholic learning center there, and the practice of posting papers on the door for discussion. And equally important, we know the actual text of his ninety-five theses (or challenges to the established church teachings).

Likewise, we may not know all of Dr. King's actions during his stay in the Birmingham jail, but we have numerous pieces of evidence from newspapers and letters *corroborating* his incarceration.

The life of Jesus of Nazareth is also attested by Jewish and Roman sources outside of the New Testament. Archaeological remains verify numerous locations and cultural events referenced in the Gospels—

actual primary sources for the life of Jesus. Like the accounts of Martin Luther, and Dr. King, we don't have all of the details. Most days of Christ's life are not recorded—but we have enough information from various spheres of evidence to call the biblical accounts truthful and historical. Like the other examples above, we know the essence of his significance in history. (See Figure 1 below and Figure 2, p. 33.)

Reliability

In order to determine what is indeed fact—true in the historical record—historians first ascertain if the source of the information is trustworthy. Is it historically reliable? *Historical reliability depends on both authenticity of sources and their accuracy.* Is an ancient text, for example, actually from the stated time period—or firmly based on a version from that period? And, does it accurately describe events in question? The ancient copies are commonly called *primary sources* because they are contemporary with historical events or fairly represent such original documents. You might find them in a museum or manuscript room, or you might read a responsible copy in an anthology.[5]

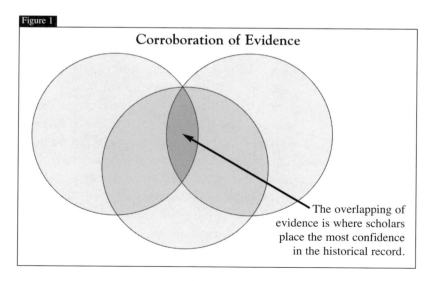

Figure 1

Corroboration of Evidence

The overlapping of evidence is where scholars place the most confidence in the historical record.

Through centuries of identifying and researching reliable sources, historians have a rich reservoir from which to draw — and the *corroboration of evidence* helps to determine truthfulness. There could exist numerous types of evidence, such as literature, personal records, archaeology, interviews of witnesses, laws, tradition and geography (see Figure 2, p. 33).

Authenticity

Authenticity is central to historical studies and applies to a wide variety of sources, ranging from manuscripts and personal items to monuments and buildings. Scholars are becoming increasingly aware of the need to distinguish authentic items from forgeries. One of history's most infamous forgeries, the "Donation of Constantine," was utilized by the Roman Catholic Church for hundreds of years before Lorenzo Valla revealed its false origins in 1440. The document erroneously credits a land gift to a relationship between Emperor Constantine and Pope Sylvester (A.D. 314-35), awarding the latter "large privileges and rich possessions." The document became known as the "False Donation of Constantine," and "is without doubt a forgery, fabricated somewhere between the years 750 and 850."[6]

Burial artifacts are extremely helpful in our knowledge of ancient civilizations. This one artifact (pictured here in The Field Museum, Chicago) is corroborated by thousands of others to give us a steady picture of Egyptian religion, politics, and economics.

Such schemes survive to the present among leading scholars, fooling prominent institutions. In 1990 one of the world's leading curators, Nicholas Turner, joined other curators in producing a British Museum exhibit entitled, "Fake? The Art of Deception."[7] The J. Paul Getty Museum in Los Angeles hired him away from London in 1994, but was embarrassed when he discovered it had spent more than one million dollars on forged Renaissance drawings between 1988 and 1992. The Mormon Church hierarchy also spent a fortune when it purchased potentially damaging documents credited to Joseph Smith.

These proved to be forgeries from one of its own members—an antiquities dealer who nearly fooled the federal government as well, a story well-documented in books such as *Salamander* and *The Mormon Murders*.[8] One of the favorite regular exhibits at the Toledo Museum of Art is "From the Vault." This contains several forgeries and an intriguing display on how researchers discovered the hoaxes.

The Brooklyn Museum has a magnificent stone bust of an Egyptian pharaoh which was originally dated to the time of the biblical Exodus (*ca.* 1440–1270 B.C.). Thousands of visitors have viewed this alleged Nile trophy now much closer to the Hudson River. However, its status has changed from centerpiece to discussion piece. After proudly displaying the bust for decades as a major artifact among the museum's Egyptian collection, researchers discovered that a noted forger had been involved in the purchase many years earlier. This revelation prompted research to determine its authenticity. That is, was it an actual bust carved by the ancient Egyptians?

The first startling discovery was that the bust was not Egyptian granite but a material native to the Black Sea region (quite a trek from the Nile). Furthermore, the tools used to drill the pharaoh's pupils were not ancient diamond-tipped bits. Instead, metal shavings from a modern drill bit were discovered deep in the eyeholes. The bust is not authentic. It is a forgery—a modern lie intended to deceive serious scholars of antiquity. For decades both scholars and casual learners based a small amount of their understanding of ancient Egypt's pharaohs on a source that is not authentic—one that is not truthful.

"Historians study sources that tell them about the past, and they write because they see something in these sources that needs to be explained."[9] Egyptian politics and religious developments are indeed of interest to a wide assortment of scholars and audiences, which makes the reliability of sources all the more crucial. Although there are numerous forgeries, there remain volumes and museums filled with reliable sources. The museums mentioned above have many thousands of artifacts that shed light on the past. For example, the Brooklyn Museum also contains the Wilbour Papyrus Collection which brings fascinating insights into ancient culture. Scholars find the collection helpful in understanding the biblical account of Joseph being sold into slavery. The Wilbour Papyrus has a similar account from around the same time and location—and mentions "Asiatics" (an ancient classification for Semitic people such as Joseph and his family). Both sets of texts, the Wilbour and the Bible, are reliable sources and help to gain a fuller understanding of the past.

Historical Accuracy

While the first question of authenticity involves the source's origin, the second question of accuracy can be applied in two ways: to the transmission or copying of an authentic text, and to a description of an event within an authentic text. Textual comparison is crucial in determining *transmission accuracy*. We might ask, for example, "Does a copy of the book of Isaiah copied by the Masoretic priests (ninth century A.D.) match a copy found among the Dead Sea Scrolls dating to around 200 B.C.?" Yes—the Masoretic text of the Middle Ages is a very close copy of the Dead Sea version, and it is the basis of many versions of the Old Testament used today. In other words, the Masoretic version has transmission accuracy. It is a responsible copy of an authentic text.[10]

Next is the question of *historical accuracy*. Is the text true to the events described?

If sources always told the truth, the historian's job would be much easier—and also rather boring. But sources, like witnesses in a murder case, often lie. Sometimes they lie on purpose, telling untruths to further a specific ideological, philosophical, or political agenda. Sometimes they lie by omission, leaving out bits of information that are crucial to interpreting an event. Sometimes sources may mislead unintentionally; the author was not aware of all the facts, or misinterpreted the facts, or was misinformed. Many are biased, either consciously or unconsciously and contain unstated assumptions; all reflect the interests and concerns of their authors. In any case, historians' sources often conflict; two different sources may tell two different stories. As a result, one of the challenges . . . is evaluating the reliability and usefulness of your sources.[11]

KEY TERMS:

Accurate: 1) A term used in connection with the transmission of texts signifying that the words of the copy closely resemble the original, or; 2) A description of the past that reflects the essence of the historical account—the description has truthfulness.

Authentic: A record or artifact that is primary—from the actual time period associated with its historical purpose.

Corroboration: The use of additional evidence to strengthen or support a knowledge base.

Empirical History: An oral or written account of the past based on experiment, evidence and/or experience.

Fact: A statement or information known with reasonable certainty to be truthful—it actually happened.

Fiction: An imaginary statement, account or information that itself is not truthful; it may reflect the essence of truthful accounts or it may be void of all historical notions.

Historical: Something from the past considered actually to have existed or occurred; the information represents reality.

Primary Sources: Records or artifacts present at the time of the event, or recorded by participants in the event, or recorded by people in contact with these participants.

Secondary Sources: Historical accounts based on a study of primary sources.

Tertiary Source: Historical accounts based on a study of secondary sources.

Truthfulness: The level of accuracy of a historical account— the account matches reality; this usually implies agreement with credible sources

If an ancient manuscript is indeed *authentic*, an actual artifact, or an ancient replica and has *transmission accuracy*, it still might not be historically reliable. That is, it might not be true to history—lacking historical accuracy. The writer or patron may have intended to promote a particular agenda or perhaps made mistakes in recounting events.

We observed that some sources' main purpose was deception, and the common classification of such items is *forgery*. In these cases they fail the test of authenticity. Other texts intended to deceive are more problematic. They lack *historical accuracy* in some places, but remain important historical documents and have proven reliable on many fronts. For example, many of the pharaohs struck their predecessors' names from memorials and added their own names. They took credit for great accomplishments; some that occurred before they were even born. Historians realize the impossibility for a pharaoh living in the twelfth century B.C. to have led a battle that numerous other sources correctly date to the fifteenth century B.C.

The vast majority of our written texts and historical artifacts are reliable, but all should be subject to scrutiny. Most colleges utilize Herodotus' *Histories* to learn about the Persians and Egyptians, but his text also contains problematic information. For example, his description of the Persian Wars is invaluable in understanding

Cuneiform clay letter and envelope. Ur III vintage reproduction owned by Jerry Pattengale, personal collection.

the sequence of events between the Greeks and Persians. However, he also notes that Xerxes led one million Persians to Greece—a figure that is commonly footnoted as a gross exaggeration. Similar footnotes often follow the biblical account of the Exodus, implying the question "Were there really six million Hebrews who marched through the desert?" Various explanations are given for this number, ranging from ancient nuances to translation miscues. Nonetheless, empirical history calls for the same examination of the Exodus details as the Herodotus account. We have similar discrepancies today, but for easily detectable reasons. For example, news accounts of interest group marches on Washington D.C. vary drastically. A promoter may claim a million in attendance while professional demographers using photo guidelines estimate a crowd one-third the size. (See Appendix Two: The Corroboration of Evidence: The Case Study of the Mysterious Pharaoh, p. 39.)

One of the more fascinating "historical accuracy" cases related to Mesopotamian and Old Testament history is the account of Sennacherib and his attack on Jerusalem. He produced a stone stele that boasts about his military feats. Sennacherib was leader of the Assyrian empire whose center of power was in the area of Nineveh north of Babylon. In 722 B.C. the Assyrians conquered the northern part of Palestine—the northern kingdom of Israel, including its capital in Samaria. The troops then moved through much of the southern kingdom known as Judah. They sacked all of the major cities except the capital of Jerusalem.

Archeological evidence attests to these Assyrian campaigns and corroborates much of Sennacherib's claims. For example, at the city of Lachish near Jerusalem, archaeologists found a cache of ostraca (broken pot shards) written by the local citizens asking for help against these invaders. Various Assyrian artifacts were also found at Lachish. The challenge to Sennacherib's accuracy comes, however, when he boasts of taking the treasures from the Jerusalem temple. In the same passage he boasts of hemming King Hezekiah in his city "like a bird in a cage." The strong implication is that he crushed the city like the rest of those on his list, including Lachish. This Assyrian boast does not match the historical evidence on a couple of accounts.

Sennacherib, King of Assyria, inscribed the details of his eight military campaigns on this hexagonal clay prism. He boasts of conquering Judah (ca. 686 B.C.), though a corroboration of the evidence shows that he failed to take Jerusalem.

The walls around modern Jerusalem date to the Turkish period, and are several feet above the ancient walls and ruins. The much smaller city from Hezekiah's time shared some of the same temple area (marked today by mosques), but was outside of the current walls.

First, there is no evidence of an Assyrian conquest of Jerusalem at this or any other time. This lack of evidence in itself is not proof, but it is suspect, especially in the light of overwhelming evidence that the city thrived until King Nebuchadnezzar and the Babylonians conquered it in 586 B.C. Sennacherib's account is also suspect when placed alongside the biblical narrative (2 Kings 18:13–16; 19:5–37; 20:20). The latter appears more consistent with the historical evidence surrounding the fate of Jerusalem.

In the biblical narrative there are numerous place names, events, and names that are attested in other accounts, including the Sennacherib stele—the earlier example of Lachish, the thirty talents of gold, the temple treasures, the mention of Hezekiah, and the conflict itself. But there are also some variations between the Assyrian and biblical account, such as the amount of silver. Sennacherib boasts of eight hundred talents, the Bible says three hundred. Some scholars note this as further evidence of boasting, others as a difference in measurement systems. Either way, it's a difference that at this point cannot be reconciled—but both mention the taking (or giving) of silver. Look more closely at Sennacherib's boast of "hemming the king in like a bird in a cage." In an attempt to demean Hezekiah, he actually validates Hezekiah's actions as recorded in the Old Testament. This is a euphemistic way of saying that although he surrounded Jerusalem he either did not or could not take it. This prompts the question of how he acquired the treasures if he was not able to take the city? The Bible notes that Hezekiah sent these to him while he was still at Lachish, then changed his mind about surrender.

At the end of the biblical account of Hezekiah, mention of his water tunnel is made. This long, hewn tunnel is a favorite tourist stop in the oldest remains of Jerusalem and it contains an inscription directly linking it to Hezekiah. The tunnel assisted the inhabitants of Jerusalem during times of siege by providing water inside the city walls.

The multiple sources surrounding Sennacherib's campaigns help to determine if the biblical texts are historically reliable. When sources are determined to be authentic and accurate, whether in part or in whole, they become part of the larger historical study—the corroboration of sources. (For a similar case study see Appendix Three: "Our Father's House" p. 43.)

The above examples demonstrate that a systematic evaluation and use of sources establish a reliable picture of the past. One might say, our only picture. Authentic and accurate sources from a variety of fields overlap to inform us— and we're left with a common corpus of information or "what is." To proceed to "why it is this way and not otherwise," we need to form hypotheses and test them. Appendix Four gives reasonable guidelines for doing so (pp. 47-49).

The Dead Sea Scrolls were found in these jars in the caves at Qumran.

Let us conclude that if a source is leading you to a fuller and more accurate understanding of past events, it is not only historically reliable, but helpful. The question then becomes one of value. Is this information significant? We live in a culture that thrives increasingly on insignificant information, whether fact or fiction.

Modern Trends and History

Postmodernism

Regardless of the preponderance of historical evidence, some people challenge major historical events or paint an inaccurate picture of them—they create "revised" or "deconstructed" accounts that are unhistorical. We live in an age of Postmodernism—an era in which some historians teach that it is permissible to create history through our research biases. In such a scheme, objectivity is illusive. Postmodernists contend that we give new meanings to what we discover from the past. They argue that our current world is too different from a remote antiquity and therefore the latter is unknowable. In *The Killing of History*, Keith Windschuttle argues that during the 1990s,

> ... the newly dominant theorists within the humanities and social sciences assert that it is impossible to tell the truth about the past or to use history to produce knowledge in any objective sense at all. They claim we can only see the past through the perspective of our own culture and, hence, what we see in history are our own interests and concerns reflected back at us. The central point upon which history was founded no longer holds: there is no fundamental distinction any more between history and myth.[12]

Contrary to the postmodern thought described above, Windschuttle's key notion is that traditional or "empirical" history can use evidence from the past to reconstruct it responsibly, and that faddish, "theory-driven" approaches fail to do so. A postmodernist philosophy of history is only

Chart 1

ERAS OF THOUGHT:

The following are general categories of thought that dominated prominent civilizations. The time parameters are more fluid than any timeline suggests, and no era contained only one approach. However, the categories do help to understand the flow of key philosophical shifts and to frame a discussion of major trends in thought. Keep in mind that the Biblical narrative and church history took place amongst these ebbs and flows.

Ancient: **Magical Worldview** "I can explain much of my world in reference to incantations, formulas and the fate of the gods"

Turning Point — Invention of writing

Time & — 3500 BC to 509 BC

Dominant Civilizations — Sumer (Mesopotamia) to Greek dominance and Early Roman Republic

Authority — Pantheon of gods

Outlook — Fatalistic—rested on the "fate" of the gods; "Everything is out of my control"

Concern — Appeasement of gods—"We must please the supernatural force(s)."

Icon — Temple

Biblical History — Post flood (pre-patriarchs) to post-Babylonian exile

Classical: **Theological Worldview** "I can explain much of my world in reference to God (or gods)"

Turning Point — Roman Expansion (expulsion of Etruscans)

Time & — 509 BC to AD 1517

Dominant Civilizations — Greece and Rome to Holy Roman Empire

Authority — Texts (Greco-Roman classics and Bible) and then the Christian Church

Outlook — Fatalistic & then Paternalistic—rested in church leaders

Concern — Orthodoxy—"We must hold to correct teaching."

Icon — Fortress—whether castle or cathedral, represents protection

Biblical & Church History — Nehemiah to Papal States and first English Bibles

Modern: **Scientific Worldview** "I can explain much of my world in reference to the laws of nature"

Turning Point — Martin Luther and 95 Theses

Time & — 1517 to 1981

Dominant Civilizations — England and France to Eastern Europe and the U.S.

Authority — Reason & Scientific Investigation

Outlook — Optimistic—"We can solve problems with technology and science"

Concern — Liberalism—"We must be tolerant of other views."

Icon — Machine

Church History — Protestant denominations form to Evangelicalism

Postmodern: **Chaotic Worldview** "I can't explain my world to others; it only has meaning for me or no meaning at all" (Nihilism)

Turning Point — Fall of the Berlin Wall

Time & — 1981 to present

Dominant Civilizations — England and France to United States

Authority — None: relativism replaces authority

Outlook — Pessimistic—"Everyone needs to look out for one's self."

Concern — Individual Expression—"Live and let live mindset."

Icon — Computer

Church History — Church growth outside the U.S. & liberal trends within the U.S.

Source: Clarence Bence, Scott Burson, Bradley Garner, David Leitzel, Jerry Pattengale, Robert Thompson, Burton Webb, "Becoming World Changers: Christianity and Contemporary Issues" (Marion: Indiana Wesleyan University 2005.)

one of these many theory-driven approaches, but remains a significant contender in literature and education. This school of thought began developing around the time of the fall of Communism and continues to hold sway in the twenty-first century. The chart of historical periods outlines some of the characteristics of philosophical shifts throughout history (see Chart 1).

Hippocrates, the father of medicine (fifth century B.C.), gave advice to Greek doctors that is also germane to the task of today's historians:

> In Medicine one must pay attention not to plausible theorizing but to experience and reason together . . . I agree that theorizing is to be approved, provided that it is based on facts, and systematically makes its deductions from what is observed . . . But conclusions drawn by the unaided reason can hardly be serviceable; only those drawn from observed facts.[13]

The Postmodern Era creates some special challenges for empirical history and poses threats to the belief in Christianity. For a historian, the issues of objective inquiry and using rational conclusions remain important, but the historian benefits from an awareness of the postmodern mindset—trying to make connections with the audience without compromising methodology. Likewise, the "opportunities" for Christianity are points of entrance for discussion. For example, the first special feature of *A History of World Civilizations from a Christian Perspective* covers ancient religions. Today's fascination with spirituality prompted this inclusion. While the reader may be more interested than earlier generations in spiritual matters, the historian hopes that the reader's interest will lead to a study of religious origins and their primary texts. For the Christian historian, providing a fuller understanding of religions through objective research helps the reader to make more sense of subjective experiences and personal choices. Belief in Christianity is a matter outside of historical science, but historical inquiry can benefit one's understanding of religion.

Chart 2

The Threats of Postmodernity to Christianity	The Opportunities of Postmodernity for Christianity
The rejection of absolute truth	Overconfidence in human reason and technology is broken
Truth becomes private interpretation. There is only truth for the individual.	Closed-system naturalism is called into question
Spirituality is unrelated to Scripture and doctrine	Spirituality is now an acceptable pursuit
Moral standards are obsolete	Moral relativism makes supernaturalism more desirable
Intensity of experience replaces depth of meaning	Common experiences provide an avenue for discussion of common meanings.

Chart 2 provides manageable categories for discussing Postmodernism, though the threats and opportunities of Postmodernism are rather complex. In the spirit of this *Brief Guide*'s thesis, we should seek to have an informed and open look at Postmodernism, such as James K. A. Smith's observations in *Who's Afraid of Postmodernism?: Taking Derrida, Lyotard, and Foucault to Church*.[14] He argues that the Church would benefit from dissecting the works of these three fathers of Postmodernism—not that he agrees with their philosophical answers but in their questions of Modernism. For Smith, the challenge is to use these thinkers' assessment to determine how far the Church itself has become more Modern than Biblical.

Perhaps we can benefit in a number of ways by taking a closer look at the founders of Postmodernist philosophy (not to be confused with Postmodern culture, as Smith notes, it is a catch-all phrase blamed for many ills). Jacques Derrida (d. 2004, the "father of Deconstruction") might help the Church to understand its most effective approach to a Postmodern culture, or to understand the Postmodern look for "alternate meanings" in texts in order to resolve opposite positions on issues. Likewise, Smith argues that through studying Jean-Francois Lyotard

(d. 1998) the Church should capitalize on telling the biblical story in an age needing a believable metanarrative. Likewise, Robert E. Webber argues that though he finds little agreement with Postmodernists the Christian metanarrative is true for the whole world.[15] Since Francois argues that singular events cannot be understood by rational theory, Webber and Smith contend that perhaps the Church should be more aggressive in telling society the mysteries and miracles associated with its religion. Likewise, perhaps Michele Foucault's (d. 1984) mantra that "power is knowledge" might help the Church understand the plight of the oppressed, especially in the light of modern case studies.

However, readers of Smith's book should come to the discussion table only after a basic reading of the Postmodern menu—its key tenets. Core knowledge is essential for this deeper look into its interaction with the Church. Readers exercising objective inquiry will likely find actual oppositions between the three Postmodernists' positions and orthodox Christianity. While Deconstructionists might call readers to question all statements and to reject moralistic discussions of standards and norms, the Christian reader likely has determined that Biblical doctrine is built on standards and the doctrine of "sin" is diametrically opposed to many relativistic claims. *Who's Afraid of Postmodernism* might help reaffirm that oppositions should not be dismissed out-of-hand. Perhaps readers will find Smith's work influenced by the great Dutch theologian, Abraham Kuyper, who emphasized Augustine's notion that "all truth is God's truth," and finding what Postmodernists have brought to light about God's creation.[16] However, readers should at the least find in Smith a challenge to take an objective look at the Church.

In his review of this *Brief Guide* manuscript, David Riggs presented a helpful caution. His reminder that James K. A. Smith "is primarily concerned with how these critiques [by Postmodernists] can help Christians to recognize the degree to which today's church has become conformed to the delusions and idolatries of modernism. In other words, he hopes that the basic critiques of postmodernist philosophy . . . can challenge us to rethink what it means for the church to be the church."[17] Smith suggests that the Postmodernists' critiques might serve as catalysts for provoking dialogue that will

19

help the church reform itself, but not as teachings that should be co-opted, such as the approach taken by the "Emergent Church."[18]

The Emerging or Emergent Church is one of many responses by Christians to cultural influences throughout history. Chart 1 provides an overview of key eras of thought to help clarify historical trends and the unfolding of dominant worldviews in history. Robert E. Webber provides an outline of the Western Church's response to these worldviews, and finds six paradigms that could be superimposed on Chart 1 as well (see p. 16). His outline includes the following six paradigms:[19]

1. 0-100 A.D. The Primitive Church, or *Biblical Paradigm*, which built on its Old Testament heritage and was preoccupied with worship and rites for the preservation and spreading of the faith.

2. 100-600 A.D. The *Ancient Paradigm*, in which Classical Christianity formed in response to Neo-Platonic thought; and the mysteries of the faith found meaning.

3. 600-1500 A.D. *The Medieval Paradigm* and the formation of a distinct Roman Christianity; based on the Aristotelian emphasis of the created order and role of institutions such as the Roman Church.

4. 1500-1750 A.D. *The Reformation Paradigm*, which built on the role of the individual's pursuit of truth (fueled by Nominalism's emphasis on the mind); the Scripture-based approach gave rise to Protestantism and denominations.

5. 1750-1980 A.D. *The Modern Paradigm* with its emphasis on reason and empirical method—a time which led liberal Christians to deny supernatural events and conservative Christians who sought "evidence that demands a verdict."

6. 1980 to the present. *The Postmodern Paradigm* which emphasizes community, evasiveness of knowledge, symbol, mystery, finds all things interrelated, and recognizes competing narratives—none offering a universal truth and no universal worldview. For the Postmodern thinker everything is relative and history is not linear but each epoch and people are understood only within their own culture.

Webber's categories vary from those in Chart 1 (see p. 16), such as dividing Modern into Reformation and Modern, nonetheless we are left with a helpful context for understanding primary and secondary sources throughout history.

This *Brief Guide* text, though written during the Postmodern era, does not imbibe relativistic notions. Instead, this writer contends that actual historical records are knowable through research. Whether the historian is of the Christian faith, of another faith, or of no faith at all, there are conclusions and experiences that can be reached in common. Historian George Marsden calls this the common sense approach. Through careful investigation of most subjects, historians can be reasonably convinced of what actually transpired.

Relativism and Sensationalism

Relativism has become the sister of sensationalism — a popular tandem ushering in the twenty-first century. In the face of overwhelming evidence, some scholars still choose to ignore or reject claims of very reliable sources about significant events, sources such as the biblical narratives. Likewise, some Christian researchers also fall into this trap — such as those who unabashedly accepted as fact the recent "James ossuary" discussion. An antiquities dealer

First-century ossuary similar to the "James ossuary" that references a father named Joseph and a brother named Joshua (translates Jesus). While the authenticity of the inscription on the James ossuary box is suspect, the box itself is genuine. These boxes were only used by Jews during the first-century.

in Jerusalem revealed a real first-century burial box that appeared to belong to James, the brother of Jesus. It was hailed as the most sensational find in a century — until a shop was discovered where the owner had falsified numerous other artifacts. While this ossuary box may indeed include an authentic inscription, as Wolfgang E. Krumbein's report suggests, it's an artifact with a storied and suspect history.[20]

Consider Stephen Hawking's *A Brief History of Time*. It hit the top of nearly all reading charts. However, this brilliant scientist captivates his readers with conjecture—which prompted numerous fictional accounts of space. His thesis and discussion about black holes and time warps represent a quantum jump to what "might be." These assertions are found in his conclusion, itself preceded by several excellent chapters of substance. Like *The Da Vinci Code* mentioned in the next section, enough accurate information lures confidence in unfounded statements. Hawking's work is indeed "sensational."[21] The Nobel Prize Committee, though recognizing Hawking as a prominent scientist, considered his work on black holes and time travel as unreliable for scientific inquiries—it is sensational speculation.

We live in an era when people thrive on tabloids and gossip columns—making discussions of objectivity like this all the more important. Our culture has selective listening; truth has been relegated to relativity while sensationalism remains the preoccupation of the masses. It would be helpful to keep the following caution in mind:

Model of the first century temple also known as "Herod's Temple" since he paid for its construction. The model resides in Jerusalem.

Relative truth is not reality, nor is sensational information (even if true) always synonymous with significant information.

In *A Student's Guide to History*, Jules R. Benjamin notes, "The main difficulty facing historians is not eliminating unanswerable or unimportant questions but choosing among the important ones."[22]

Other Challenges
to Empirical History

Folly: In addition to postmodern accounts, there are those that go considerably beyond a loose interpretation or revision of the facts — they blatantly reject evidence and offer totally unfounded conclusions. Most historians quickly dismiss these preposterous accounts as folly.

It remains unfortunate that such accounts still attract sizeable followings. For example, several people postulate that astronauts never really landed on the moon and that scientists faked it.[23] This line of reasoning surfaced in the plot of *Capricorn One* (1978), a story about NASA faking a trip to Mars and then creating a cover up. Though made for entertainment purposes, *Capricorn One* heightened belief in alternate theories of space reality. Likewise, numerous publications have highlighted a problematic space theory that credits aliens with building the pyramids. This preposterous assertion by Erich Von Daniken was popularized in the documentary, *Chariots of the Gods*.

Evidential fabrication: Even more startling than these bizarre space accounts are the false notions about Christianity in the first runaway best-selling novel of the twenty-first century — *The Da Vinci Code*. It has already sold over twelve million copies. The Holy Grail, according to novelist Dan Brown, is not Christ's chalice from the Last Supper but Mary Magdalene's womb. According to Brown, she bore Christ's child. He espouses a wide assortment of self-proclaimed "truths" in his book's storyline, even qualifying them as "facts" in the book's foreword. This fabrication of evidence to support a theory is similar to the "False Donation of Constantine" scandal. However, in *The Da Vinci Code* the benefit went to an author and publishing house instead of clerics and an institution, and the erroneous documents were immediately identified by scholars worldwide. His sensational plot managed to win the day with the reading public, but not an objective inquiry.

Fascinating storylines, engaging writing, and confident assertions give the text a veneer of credibility. However, numerous scholars quickly peeled back this flimsy attempt to recreate history in a modern image.[24] Brown simply spins a thrilling story—a fictional tale with enough historical information intertwined to make the false information appear believable. *The Da Vinci Code* is fiction. The essence of the historical accounts are ignored or altered beyond recognition.

Unlike fictional novels, credible history texts follow standard practices to ensure reliability. It is important to apply the same standards to all sources, including the biblical texts—key sources in any "Christian perspective" of history.

Democratization of knowledge: A new set of standards is emerging among the cyberspace audiences, a development that likely creates the most significant challenge to objective inquiry—"group think" or "consensus knowledge" like that found in Wikipedia. This product of wiki-reality endorses "open-source ethics" and "radical collaboration," a process that "allows any Web surfer to edit its articles." Its 30,000 official members are anonymous "editors," and the entries reflect consensus decisions. Taken by itself, this approach sounds reasonable—but many of these entries contain uniformed representations of subjects. Few "authorities" are involved in the process (1,000 of its 30,000 editors).[25]

One of the foundations of the academy and the long history of organized education is responsible peer review. Higher education and responsible reporters designate an "authority" or "scholar" as one who has demonstrated a mastery of information available on a given subject. This competency is evaluated through structured peer review and formal credentialing processes. This does not negate the value of open-source approaches, but it does present a caution for accepting them as authoritative. This very caution is why one of Wikipedia's founders, Larry Sanger, became a critic of his own invention and started Citizendium, from "citizen's compendium." Sanger "plans to create for the site a 'representative democracy,' in which self-appointed experts [invited by the site's organizers] oversee the editing and shaping of articles." While there remain open-source contributions by any Web surfer, only scholars with "the qualifications typically needed for a tenure track-academic position" will edit the site.[26]

If Citizendium is to be successful, by its own designer's admission, then its gatekeepers will be those who have proven abilities of objectively researching sources and coming to reliable and unbiased conclusions. The "tenure-track" process is based on this premise of responsible scholarship, and most of the 4,500 American universities include rigorous steps in attaining tenure.

Traditional education is dealing with many changes and global access to knowledge is reshaping economies and influencing foreign policy. Concomitantly, the pursuit of objective inquiry remains a constant need for meaningful discourse.[27] Its principles transcend mediums.

A Stanford University dean recently challenged the value of "old-school assignments" in this *Google* age, such as memorizing the names of South American rivers.[28] However, classroom educators note the students' struggle with evaluating *Googled* information and their students' failure to ascertain reliability. The Curriki.org site is attempting to help teachers with this validity problem through its open-source curricula for K-12, built by teachers globally; but it still begs the question of objective inquiry for learners. Successful analysis requires us to build on our core knowledge while processing new information using our portable skills—"critical thinking, making connections between ideas and knowing how to keep on learning." Objective inquiry, itself a portable skill, is especially important at a time when half of today's high school seniors and new collegians cannot "correctly judge the objectivity of a website"—the key source of their information.[29]

Keeping Fiction in
Historical Perspective

Most mornings this writer greets Frank Peretti in the large rotunda outside my office. His bronze bust marks his place in "The Society of World Changers," an honor for having over twelve million books in print including *This Present Darkness* and *The Oath*. They capture readers' imagination about spiritual warfare—a cataclysmic fight between angels and demons that reflects biblical prophecy. These fictional stories prompted millions to consider biblical warnings, and readers (including me) to reflect seriously on their prayer lives. Nonetheless, these novels' popularity raised alarm when some religious groups based prayer manuals on them and also classified Peretti as an authority on the New Age movement.[30]

Fiction, from the Latin *fingere,* "to shape or form," intrigues us through its ability to deal with complex issues. During the first week of 2007, Mitch Albom's *One More Day* topped *The New York Times* Best Seller List. Like his former bestseller, *The Five People You Meet in Heaven,* and the works of Peretti, an engaging style, character development and plot prompt reflection about the real world, and often about our place in it. Because of our ability to think both creatively and objectively, fiction has had an important role in civilizations since the beginning of written texts—from ancient Egypt's *Tale of Sinuhe*, the Sumerian account

Early Mesopotamian civilizations created a series of gods and mythical stories; these gods became the fulcrum of their social order as depicted in this divine tribute on an economic text.

of Enkidu and the Greek classic, *Lysistrata* (411 B.C.), to *The Pilgrim's Progress* (1678), *Candide* (1759), *Pride and Prejudice* (1815) and *The Scarlet Letter* (1850). This is perhaps illustrated best in American history in the opus of Harriett Beecher Stowe, *Uncle Tom's Cabin* (1852). Abraham Lincoln allegedly greeted her with such an appraisal of the events leading to the Civil War, saying "So this is the little lady who made this big war."

In 1993, *The Chronicle of Higher Education* noted that the top ten reading list of American collegians contained almost all fiction titles.[31] The sensational *Jurassic Park* was the most-read book. Among the others were four John Grisham titles and Dr. Seuss' *Oh, the Places You'll Go*. Although these books are intriguing, and some are captivating, they are about what "could be." For the most part, they are entertainment, and obviously this list reflects the students' cross-discipline break from textbooks, an escape from the heavier collegiate reading. However, the list differs little from those at major bookstores and the media in general, and what is currently happening in high schools and colleges. Fictional characters appear on screens, billboards, lunch boxes, notebooks, and T-shirts across the nation.

Good fiction can be motivating and thought provoking. It helps people to dream, to have vision, and perhaps to make some otherwise unthinkable contribution to humankind. Readers often finish books with a renewed passion for justice or a new insight into important issues—books such as, *My Name is Asher Lev, Animal Farm*, and *The Outsiders*. Likewise, some viewers exit theaters energized for a task at hand. *The Emperor's Club, The Mission, Mr. Holland's Opus*, and *Dead Poet's Society* all challenge us to a higher level of work—to be a world changer, to cry "Carpe Diem!" But we need to be careful to remain visionaries and not *fictionaries*. Our designs and worldviews should be firmly planted in truth.[32]

Some say that art and fictional works are lies that tell the truth. In many cases, this is probably true. Chaim Potok's depiction of Asher Lev prompts readers to envision his house, his crucifix painting, and his mom and dad standing in the window. This imagery tells the truth about the human condition, about struggles to find fulfillment. The caution here is that our admiration for the brilliant writing and beautiful "lies" never eclipses our recognition of and engagement with truth. The truth may be principles that assist us with emotional struggles or it might be historical accounts of world changers, like Jesus Christ.

In *Why We Read Fiction*, one of Lisa Zunshine's key observations is about our interest in determining fact from fiction. She notes that research sheds light on "readers'" enduring preoccupation with the thorny issue of the 'truth' of literary narrative and the distinction between 'history' and 'fiction.'" She aptly notes that fiction enables us to pattern our thoughts in "newly nuanced" ways, allowing for new application of learning to our lives.[33]

As we pursue objective inquiry, we occasionally need to stand back from the Venn diagram of overlapping sources and remind ourselves that the information before us enables us to enjoy fiction, and fiction helps us to appreciate facts. Like *The Matrix*, we're constantly challenged to separate the real from the unreal. However, in stark contrast to this brilliant fictional account we all have the opportunity to determine what is truthful.

This is a close up of the seal impression from the above cuneiform text. In addition to showing respect for local gods, these seal impressions were like signatures, depicting the author. Several large caches of these clay texts were found in Mesopotamia, including the Nineveh library of Ashurbanipal—the last great king of the Assyrians—and large finds in Ebla and Uruk (biblical Erech). By comparing thousands of extant texts, many aspects of ancient culture surface. Likewise, this knowledge base also helps to detect forgeries—for example, stylus strokes ceased beginning from the right from the Old Babylonian period forward.

The Importance of Comparing Historical Records

We have discussed some of the key issues in establishing the historical record and have found remarkable hand-in-glove fits involving biblical and external (or extra-biblical) sources. All historical studies, biblical and otherwise, should follow the same standards, and source corroboration is the sensible way to arrive at a reliable interpretation of past events.

Many studies stem from contradictory interpretations or opposing claims. For example, at the Nuremberg trials, some of the infamous Nazi leaders pleaded innocent to heinous crimes—but the abundance of evidence did not *corroborate* their testimonies. Thus, they were summarily hanged and responsible world civilization books represent the whole picture. President Nixon proclaimed before millions that he was telling the truth, yet tapes, testimonies, and files proved him to be a liar. He resigned in disgrace. Likewise, consider the millions of people who died as a result of Chairman Mao's "Great Leap Forward" and "Cultural Revolution." His claims of economic self-sufficiency, proclaimed by his own pen, were completely discredited by various other sources which reflect the bleak reality of an economic pandemic.[34] To read his *Little Red Book* and "official" Communist accounts of these events without reading a sampling of the thousands of other sources from this era would be grossly misinforming.

In each of the above cases, scholars and/or judges used an assortment of evidence to determine what actually transpired in order to determine which of the opposing claims were true. Underlying this international judicial process was the value of sound logic, especially the Law of Non-Contradiction.[35] This central principle of logic is attributed to Aristotle and asserts:

> *Two opposing views cannot both be true at the same time and in the same respect.*[36]

For Postmodernists preoccupied with relative notions and the desire to find common ground among opposing views, it is no surprise that a law that eliminates some claims as credible finds opposition. In *Mere Christianity*, C. S. Lewis employed this logic in his discussion of Christ's historical message:

> I am trying here to prevent anyone saying the really foolish thing that people often say about Him [Jesus of Nazareth]: 'I'm ready to accept Jesus as a great moral teacher, but I don't accept His claim to be God.' That is the one thing we must not say. A man who was merely a man and said the sort of things Jesus said would not be a great moral teacher. He would either be a lunatic—on a level with the man who says he is a poached egg—or else he would be the Devil of Hell. You must make your choice. Either this man was, and is, the Son of God: or else a madman or something worse. You can shut Him up for a fool, you can spit at Him and kill Him as a demon; or you can fall at His feet and call Him Lord and God. But let us not come with any patronizing nonsense about His being a great human teacher. He has not left that open to us. He did not intend to.[37]

Lewis came to this conclusion cognizant of both historical sources and sound logic. He is not claiming that sources or logic prove Christ's supernatural nature, but that historically reliable sources demonstrate clearly that Christ claimed to be supernatural (and by implication, there's reason to believe him). Lewis was answering critics of his day, but he is often cited in response to illogical conclusions by the liberal group known as The Jesus Seminar. Dr. Edwin Yamauchi directly challenges the logic of this same group by using objective inquiry (see Figure 2).

The challenge for an accurate reading of history is constantly before us. See Appendix Four: "A Look at Logic: Inference to the Best Explanation."

From the various sources of late antiquity we can construct a rather certain picture of many events and societies of the Old Testament and, with even more certainty, those of first-century Israel.[38] We are able to look through the glass of time with a surprisingly clear view of the political, social, and religious arrangements in which the Old and New Testament writers moved. This same confidence continues throughout the historical narrative of the Christian story in an increasingly "global" world.

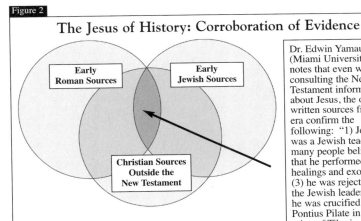

Figure 2

The Jesus of History: Corroboration of Evidence

Early Roman Sources

Early Jewish Sources

Christian Sources Outside the New Testament

Dr. Edwin Yamauchi (Miami University) notes that even without consulting the New Testament information about Jesus, the other written sources from his era confirm the following: "1) Jesus was a Jewish teacher, (2) many people believed that he performed healings and exorcisms; (3) he was rejected by the Jewish leaders; (4) he was crucified under Pontius Pilate in the reign of Tiberius; (5) despite his shameful death, his followers, who believed that he was still alive, spread beyond Palestine so that there were multitudes of them in Rome by A.D. 64; (6) all kinds of people from the cities and countryside—men and women, slave and free—worshipped him as God by the beginning of the second century."

"... The orthodox view of Jesus still stands as the most credible portrait when all of the evidence is considered, including the corroboration offered by ancient sources outside the New Testament."

Source: Edwin M. Yamauchi, "Jesus Outside the New Testament: What Is the Evidence?" *Jesus Under Fire* (Grand Rapids, MI: Zondervan Publishing House, 1995), 221-222, see 207-229.

Those finding the Scriptures trustworthy sources can also find countless other reliable sources for more recent history, and vice versa. For example, Martin Gilbert is considered the foremost authority on

Winston Churchill. His series on Churchill (1971–2000) is an accurate and brilliant account of Churchill's life. It is considered the "definitive" work on the great British statesman. However, even though it is based on the best primary collection known to exist, Gilbert himself did not serve as an

First-century synagogue remains beneath third-century synagogue wall. The bottom strata is basalt native to the Galilee region and is the synagogue in Capernaum where Jesus likely worshipped (Matthew 4). The top layer is imported stone indicating greater wealth.

eyewitness to the events. Nonetheless, his interpretation of events is consistent with the wealth of evidence from various types of sources. In one of the boldest public displays of faulty logic, Robert Faurisson published "How Historian Gilbert Falsifies and Invents" in the *Journal of Historical Review* (March 4, 1987). Through the veneer of scholarship he attempts to dismantle Gilbert's assertions about Nazi genocide. However, as Faurisson's argument unfolds, especially in the light of his various other articles to the French newspaper *Le Monde*, it becomes obvious that he is a "Holocaust denier," or as he prefers, a "Holocaust revisionist." While he might actually find some technical errors in the dozens of volumes by Gilbert, any basic corroboration of evidence about World War II reveals that Faurisson's denial of gas chambers and a systematic attempt to exterminate the Jews is nonsense. Denying the truthfulness of these events not only lacks support but rejects millions of records that corroborate these events.

Regardless of whether historic inquiry involves a religious topic, one's rejection or avoidance of truth does not nullify that truth. Millions of people throughout history have contended that the Bible contains the most important truths necessary for this life and next. Such veneration of its contents would be suspect if it lacked historical credibility. However, its stories match history and its principles for life match the realities of the human condition. The Bible is historically reliable and arguably the most significant collection of texts in history.

Appendix One

The Crossroads Principle:
"An Afro at the Crossroads"

The following article first appeared in *The Chronicle-Tribune* (2002, Marion, Indiana). The town of Weaver (originally named Crossroads) factored in the Underground Railroad route along current State Road 37. Weaver was a significant gathering place and home for African Americans until the early 1900s. Although the town has disappeared it remains a popular reunion and celebration site for families with ties to Weaver—many hundreds attend gatherings throughout the year at the site where a black Masonic temple once stood, along with an orphanage it supported. My family has been restoring the lone surviving farm from that era. Little marks the town today other than a small African Methodist Episcopal (A.M.E.) church along County Road 600 South, the cemetery mentioned in the dedication, and a small sign at the town's only crossroads (300 W). However, a nationally touring museum display on African American history featured Weaver and venerates the culture that once thrived here. These artifacts are housed at the Marion Public Library. In the context of our discussion of objective inquiry, the article below reflects the need to go beyond ascertaining truth to finding its connections to our daily lives.[39]

An Afro at the Crossroads[40]

Our 1966 Buck Creek classroom was predictable.
Kathy sitting by the radiator biting her flat eraser. Bruce drawing

Fantastic Four's Rock Man. Ned staring at the graveyard through the four-foot second-story window. Big Jim whispering to Big Ben. My cousin John passing notes. Tim sneaking a taste of Elmer's Glue.

You could always find the silver pencil sharpener mounted between the slate board and dark door trim, and the round generic clock centered above the teacher's substantial oak desk.

Glancing across the rows of flip-top desks you would see a bubbly assortment of classmates. Red hair. Blonde hair. Freckles. Quasi rich. Mostly poor. All white.

We never thought twice about the latter. That's the way it was. It was all we knew. "Diversity" may have been a word, somewhere, but not a cause or a curricular concern.

Not much changed in our neck of the woods throughout the 1960s and 70s. While Selma was sizzling with racial protests, many northern towns were conspicuously silent. Discussion on segregation and equality were for Atlanta and Little Rock, and for their teachers, politicians, and police—not for the Buck Creeks scattered throughout the rural north. At least not among elementary kids.

It would be years before we became aware of such matters.

The first non-White in any class wouldn't come until late in high school. Blacks were found in *National Geographic* and big cities. Paths between Buck Creek and *MoTown* rarely crossed.

"The only colored folks we ever saw," reflected a Buck Creek alumnus, "were the rail workers whose sleeper car pulled off the tracks here. We played 'em in softball. Watched 'em closely and they behaved themselves—perfect gentlemen. Those were memorable games."

You can imagine the buzz around Buck Creek when my sister "went and found her one of them colored men"— recounted my uncle while hunting sponge mushrooms.

I smile today at the irony of raising my family in the historic black community of Weaver, Indiana, originally called Crossroads. Faded pictures reveal a general store, three churches, a school, a landing strip for a lone crop duster, a horse track, and many social functions.

By 1920, most of the families from this community had moved a few miles north to Marion—new laws permitted them equal access to public schools. The saddest of ironies occurred in 1930. Within months of officially closing its town status, former residents witnessed in their new desegregated town the last public lynching in America. Equality in education was not synonymous with civility.

America knows of the lynching and alleged KKK strongholds twelve miles south. It also knows of James Dean's home a few miles east. Weaver is poised as a crossroads in history, and between divergent values and causes.

My four boys pass daily through the Weaver (Crossroads) intersection. On every passing their lives intersect with the history of racism and the cause of equality—a dynamic I've termed the "Crossroads Principle." When our lives personally intersect an issue or an aspect of a cause, experiential learning takes place. We have a chance to personalize the learning—what educators say is the key to a deeper understanding.

My eldest son chose Rosa Parks as the subject of a major paper. He found that the same values she held while sitting on that Alabama bus were somehow connected to our town. These values once plowed the soil of our own farm and the rest of Crossroads plots. He knows that Crossroads was more than a name for a black community. It was a need for a people's survival. It was a divergence in values.

The Crossroads Principle occurs not only for those who drive past our farm, but whenever you reflect on a class roster or the selection of curriculum. It happens when your black son brings home a white girlfriend, or when you plan a block party Friday night, forgetting your Jewish neighbor's Sabbath. It occurs when you hear a sportscaster talk about the breeding of a race for sports, an esteemed Big Ten coach apologize for inadvertent comments offending whites, or a local landlord refuse rent to a new family due to race. It's when you build a Habitat home for a former classmate.

We fly through crossroads weekly if not daily. We're occasionally blindsided. The hope is that we become more aware of the intersections, and that through these passages we better navigate the journey.

My relatives now hold reunions where the Buck Creek school stood. Recently, several families pulled from the crushed stone lot and began their homeward treks through the worn crossroad at town center. I noticed a Buck Creek boy pausing on his bicycle long enough to watch this rare flurry of traffic.

The boy's head turned to my sister's car ahead of us. My niece's wind-blown Afro filled nearly half the rear window as she turned to wave goodbye. Was the young onlooker's perspective one of curiosity of the unfamiliar, like mine forty years earlier? Was he more preoccupied with the number of cars passing than the color of the passengers? Was this serendipitous intersection with another race his only diversity crossroads, with no intentional ones at school, church or home?

We try to prepare for intersections. At times, we plan them. Perhaps we need to hand the wheel to a friend while we press our faces against the rear glass and reflect on what crossed our path.

Intentionally or unintentionally, intersections should help our introspection.

Appendix Two

The Corroboration of Evidence:
The Case Study of the Mysterious Pharaoh

In the British Museum is the famous Abydos list of Egyptian kings. Before the completion of the new museum it was located near the Rosetta Stone. The list is comprised of cartouches, the hieroglyph symbols in oval shapes, such as the ones some people wear as fashionable necklaces. However, the name of King Tutankhamen (King Tut) is missing; King Tut's cartouche is not on the list. Does it mean that because the list is an authentic artifact (nearly 3,500 years old) that it is also reliable? Far from it. A few years ago I had meetings with Dr. Zahi Hawass, head curator of the Cairo Museum in Egypt. He had just finished showing me the treasures of King Tut's tomb. I was also privileged to thumb through photo albums with one of Hawass' chief colleagues, Ramesses, the director of conservation for antiquities. He showed me numerous pictures of his team moving colossal structures from the Aswan area.[41]
The artifacts in both the Cairo and British Museums are authentic,

Ramesseum in Luxor: Head of Colossus of Ramesses II Against Osiride Pillars in Second Court, Egypt

including the kings' list. However, the list was part of a concerted effort in antiquity to erase the name of King Tut from history—due to his father's bizarre apostasy.[42]

His father, Akhenaton (also known as Amenhotep IV), had attempted to change the longstanding religious practices of Egypt by a radical implementation of the worship of a sun disc. He even moved the capital to a remote desert site, Amarna. By looking at thousands of artifacts, especially those at his father's new capital (which was posthumously buried for over two thousand years and forgotten), we are able to determine why Tut's name was omitted. The Egyptians wanted to erase his father's name and descendants from history. A lie? Call it what you may, but at the least it is an unreliable list without the context of the other finds.

Truth in History—You Make the Call

Is what you just read above historically reliable? How can you determine the answer? You could check the author's hard drive and assorted disks to match the text with his 1996 journal notes and Visa statements. The latter would also help you to decide whether he had visited Egypt and London. (You'll also find a receipt for the Greek restaurant on Coptic Street in London—great food!) You could check the kings' list—it is in numerous articles—or you could go look at the original for yourself. Also, you could take a trip to the Brooklyn Museum and ask about the Egyptian bust. (Oh, and ask to see the various Coptic forgeries as well.) Fly to Cairo and then make the trek to Karnack (much has been resituated) and Armarna (get ready for quite a ride). While you're there, see if you can track down the director of conservation for antiquities, Ramesses, and extend greetings to him and his wonderful wife, Mona. Be sure while you're in their second-floor condo to look at his amazing pictures of the dismantling and reconstruction of the colossus statue of the pharaoh—the original Ramesses. You might also find that the formal title for Dr. Hawass is now "Secretary General of the Egyptian Supreme Council of Antiquities." He has been much in the news since the discovery of the new tomb (KV 63) in the Valley of the

Kings by Dr. Otto Schaden and his University of Memphis team. You might also interview his team's epigrapher, Dr. Maraiam Ayad, who also worked with me during an excavation in the late 1990s in Wadi Natrun—which was why I was in Egypt. Our team also produced "The Odyssey in Egypt" program, another "artifact" to verify my above accounts. Another interesting development you'll discover is that the new tomb, KV 63, appears to be associated with King Tut's biological mother—otherwise ignored in Egyptian chronicles because she was the second wife of the king.

You likely get the picture. There are ways to determine if information is historically reliable. Some things are believed on faith and not challenged, such as the existence of Cairo and that there is a real brick-and-mortar museum named the British Museum. Is it because it is familiar information? Or, because people trust history books, journals, and maps? It is probably due to the numerous sources from various perspectives that give you information about Egypt and London. They "corroborate" one another.

The "Eastern" or "Golden" Gate faces the Mount of Olives and has been sealed since its completion. It is among the oldest gates, dating either to late Byzantine rule in the sixth-century A. D., or to the Umayyad caliphs a century later. Corroborating evidence immediately dates the rest of the wall late (Ottoman) due to its crenellation design and general pattern. Also, archaeologists located two earlier gates, 7 to 8 feet beneath this one, one likely dating to the time of Christ. The current gate's enclosure represents the conflicting Jewish and Islamic teachings associated with it. Muslim graves were also placed in front of the gate as a deterrent to Jewish interests. This gate exemplifies the need for interdisciplinary research, as gaining objective evidence includes fields ranging from religion and history to archaeology, cartography, architecture and languages. See Jerry Pattengale, "Beautiful Gate," *The Anchor Bible Dictionary,* David Noel Freedman, ed., vol. 1 (New York: Doubleday, 1992): 631-632; and, W. H. Mare, *The Archaeology of the Jerusalem Area* (Grand Rapids, MI: Baker Book House, 1987): 158.

Appendix Three
The Father's House[43]

As this text is being written, *U.S. News & World Report* issued a special edition entitled, "Mysteries of the Bible." This topical issue begins with a summary of a scholarly world divided over the biblical narrative. It aptly notes that "some scholars say that there is no archaeological evidence for key events in the Bible." Some contend that prominent Biblical personalities are folklore. However, major discoveries continue to surface that make positions suspect. For example, to continue to argue that King David did not exist is untenable from a scholarly position.

On July 21, 1993, the biblical King David surfaced, literally, in stone. On that date, inscribed stones were found at the ancient city of Dan. Though the basalt fragments were only part of a longer inscription, two important words stood out. When translated they read "House of David." It is the first evidence outside the Bible that King David actually existed. It is also evidence that the southern kingdom of Judah was also known by this great king. "How?" and "Why?" Judah was known as the House of David deserves a further look.

The people in ancient Israel and Mesopotamia thought of their government much like a family. They were organized with the father as the head of the nuclear family. Even as adults, his sons would look to him for protection and advice. A group of related families, often called a clan, would have one man designated as its head. The group of related clans was a tribe of which again one man was the head. He was seen as the father of the tribe. The grouping of tribes, such as the twelve tribes of Israel, saw the king as the father of the entire country. This way of looking at family and government is called the

"Patrimonial House Model" or the "House of the Father."

The title was used to understand how the actual government was viewed. It was also used as a symbol to describe certain relationships. This can be seen in situations such as competing groups for ruling as in 2 Samuel 3:6 where it states, "During the war between the house of Saul and *the house of David*, Abner had been strengthening his own position in *the house of Saul*" (NIV, emphasis mine).

Another relationship is to refer to the descendants of a person as in Amos 7:16 where God commands Amos to say, "Now then, hear the word of the Lord. You say, 'Do not prophesy against Israel, and stop preaching against *the house of Isaac*.'" (NIV, emphasis mine)

Perhaps the most encompassing view of this house designation is when the term refers to an entire kingdom. This happens especially with the southern kingdom of Judah which is often referred to as the "House of David." Although there were many dynasties in the northern kingdom, it was known as the "House of Omri." These designations are recognized not only within the community but also by other people groups. For example, Assyrian inscriptions refer to the northern kingdom of Israel as the "House of Omri."

Some have suggested that this idea of viewing the world can even be seen in the layout of houses. The head of the house, or patriarch, appears to have his wives, unmarried daughters, sons, and their wives and children all living in separate units within the family compound.

It is perhaps this very image which Jesus was using in John 14:1-3, "Do not let your hearts be troubled. Trust in God; trust also in me. In my *Father's house* are *many rooms*; if it were not so, I would have told you. I am going there to prepare a place for you. And if I go and prepare a place for you, I will come back and take you to be with me that you also may be where I am" (NIV, emphasis mine). Jesus may be using this image of the father's house in a way familiar to his disciples, but it is easily lost in cultures no longer familiar with this way of viewing the world.

When archaeologists discovered the "House of David" inscription, it not only mentioned the Israelite king but also employed common language of that era—further proof of its authenticity. The irony of this discovery is that the first external validation of David outside of the

Bible comes from Dan, a city that had constructed a golden calf shrine and blatantly opposed the religion David held so dear.

Sources:

Ben-Tor, Amnon, ed. *The Archaeology of Ancient Israel*. The Open University of Israel, 1992.

Biran, Avraham and Joseph Naveh, "An Aramaic Stele Fragment from Tel Dan," *Israel Exploration Journal*. 43 (1993): 81-98.

Holy Bible, New International Version. Grand Rapids, MI: Zondervan, 1988.

"Mysteries of the Bible," Special Edition. *U.S. News & World Report*, 2006.

Shanks, Hershel, ed. *Ancient Israel*. Biblical Archaeology Society, 1999.

Schloen, David. The House of the Father as Fact and Symbol. The President and Fellows of Harvard College, 2001.

VanGemeren, Willem A., ed. *New International Dictionary of Old Testament Theology and Exegesis* (CD ROM version). Grand Rapids, MI: Zondervan, 1999.

This view is from atop Masada ("fortress") near the Dead Sea looking down on the remains of Roman encampments. The history of Jerusalem, Qumran and Masada are all connected to the Great Jewish Revolt. Qumran fell to the Romans in A.D. 68, Jerusalem and the great (second) temple fell in A.D. 70, and Masada fell in A.D. 73. This occurred after a long siege by the Romans as noted in the works of Josephus, the Jewish historian (considered a traitor) who wrote for the Romans. The numerous finds in Jerusalem and at Qumran, along with the remains of the Roman fortifications pictured here, corroborate Josephus' account. The soldiers built a ramp up the side of Masada, a natural rock plateau that seemed impregnable. When defeat was imminent, the approximately 1,000 Jewish zealots committed suicide the night before the Roman's breached the wall. See Josephus, *The Jewish War*, VII.247-405. Josephus informs us that when the Romans entered "they came upon rows of dead bodies, they did not exult over them as enemies but admired the nobility of their resolve . . ." Today, Israeli troops hold inductive ceremonies there under the motto, "Masada shall not fall again."

Appendix Four

A Look at Logic: Inference to the Best Explanation

"Inference to the best explanation" is common to all sound inductive reasoning:

According to this approach, we begin with the evidence available to us. Then out of a pool of live options determined by our background beliefs, we select the best of various competing explanations to give an account of why the evidence is as it is and not otherwise. For the scientist, the chosen explanation constitutes his theory; for the historian, her proposed reconstruction of the past. The scientist then tests his proposed theory by performing various experiments; the historian tests her historical reconstruction by seeing how well it elucidates the evidence.[44]

Factors for Testing a Historical Hypothesis:

1. The hypothesis, together with other true statements, must imply further statements describing present, observable data.

2. The hypothesis must have greater *explanatory scope* (that is, imply a greater variety of observable data) than rival hypotheses.

3. The hypothesis must have greater *explanatory power* (that is, make the observable data more probable) than rival hypotheses.

4. The hypothesis must be more *plausible* (that is, be implied by a greater variety of accepted truths, and its negation implied by fewer accepted truths) than rival hypotheses.

5. The hypothesis must be *less ad hoc* (that is, include fewer new suppositions about the past not already implied by existing knowledge) than rival hypotheses.

6. The hypothesis must be *disconfirmed by fewer accepted beliefs* (that is, when conjoined with accepted truths, imply fewer false statements) than rival hypotheses.

7. The hypothesis must so exceed its rivals in fulfilling conditions (2) through (6) [above] that there is little chance of a rival hypothesis, after further investigation, exceeding it in meeting these conditions.[45]

Outlining Logic and Anticipating Objections

One of the best ways to understand logic in general and the use of inference to the best explanation is to study good and bad logic. For example, one could read Edwin Yamauchi's "Jesus Outside the New Testament: What Is the Evidence" and determine if his conclusions are based firmly on the information he presents. As we learned in Figure Two in this book's last chapter, Dr. Yamauchi is predictably organized in his presentation of information, which simplifies an examination of logic. He also has a long and esteemed scholarly career. In addition to his many books, over 100 articles, and various scholarship appointments, he also has demonstrated proficiency in 26 languages. Unlike Wikipedia postings, his work comes with around 50 years of peer-reviewed recognition. In other words, his look at logic comes from a recognized authority.[46]

Whether studying Yamauchi's works or those reaching contrary conclusions, it is imperative to review logical structures. For example, a quick overview of logic is found in Ed Miller's *Questions that Matter: An Invitation to Philosophy*. He provides a basic discussion of inductive and deductive reasoning, along with an accounting of the most common logical fallacies.[47] The delightful work of David Hackett Fischer, *Historians' Fallacies,* is another text rich with insight on logic—and provides hundreds of examples from actual texts.[48]

Likewise, one could learn from scholarly lectures on logic, such as Ravi Zacharias' "Logical Consistency."[49] Also, one could follow a debate and outline the evidence and chart the logic. For example, William Lane Craig debated Frank R. Zindler on the subject of "Atheism vs. Christianity: Where Does the Evidence Point."[50] The answers to the following questions will help to assess the discussion:

1. What credentials do the participants bring to the discussion table? (Are they scholars?)

2. List the evidence for each person's position.

3. Is the evidence germane to the advertised topic of discussion?

4. Do the conclusions stem from the evidence (or premises)?

5. Chart the general logic used in presenting each position.

6. Chart the specific logic used for emphasizing minor points.

7. What lessons did you learn about the stated topic?

This inscription provides the only evidence outside the New Testament that Pontius Pilate was indeed historical, a fact argued for decades by critics of the historicity of these accounts. The text reads: TIBERIEUM (PON)TIUS (PRAEF)ECTUS IUDA(EA)E. It coincides as well with other first-century evidence corroborating the veracity of these texts about Christ's journey, such as the extant tombs with a rolling stone, a "Mount of Olives" and the remains of an Eastern Gate.

Appendix Five
Deductive and Inductive Reasoning

Any attempt to utilize new knowledge gained through objective inquiry requires a continued use of sound reasoning. A responsible interpretation or reconstruction of the past depends on it. *The Foundation for Critical Thinking* defines "reasoning" in its usual candid and helpful way—"Reasoning occurs when we draw conclusions based on reasons." Put another way, reasons are the sufficient grounds for a logical conclusion. They make facts gathered through corroborative investigation intelligible. Most dictionaries will define *reason* (n., L. *ratio*, reckoning or account) as the basis for a decision. "Premise" and "reason" are often used interchangeably.

Reasoning involves a systematic comparison of facts which usually involves either the process of deduction or induction. "We can upgrade the quality of our reasoning when we understand the intellectual processes that underlie reasoning."[51]

Deductive Reasoning begins with universal truths, or put another way, argues from general principles to conclusions. A deductive argument is *"an argument form in which one reasons from premises [reasons] that are known or assumed to be true to a conclusion that follows necessarily from these premises."* The philosopher Plato endorsed this approach—arguing from universals.

Example of a deductive argument (the following is a *syllogism*—two supporting premises and a conclusion). If the premises are true, the conclusion is guaranteed.

Premise (or reason) All men are mortal
Premise (or reason) Socrates is a man
Conclusion Therefore, Socrates is a mortal

Inductive Reasoning begins with pieces of evidence and argues to a conclusion. In a sense, it's the opposite of the deductive argument form. The philosopher Aristotle championed this approach, chronicling information, or parts, to understand the whole. Inductive reasoning is *"an argument form in which one reasons from premises that are known or assumed to be true to a conclusion that is supported by the premises but does not necessarily follow from them."*[52]

Like the syllogism example above for deductive reasoning, a popular example for the inductive form is found in the Sherlock Holmes stories. In commenting on a Holmes' example, Ed Miller writes, "This is an excellent example of what goes on in inductive arguments: moving from particular facts here, analogies there, common threads and connections everywhere, to a conclusion that is suggested by all of that evidence." As we've noted throughout this text, "the more supportive the premises, the more reasonable and the higher the probability of the conclusion. Thus, as with deductive arguments, not just any old premises will do."[53]

Examples of an inductive argument (these are two common types among many). If the premises are true, the conclusion is probably true.

Universal generalization:

Instance 1 of A is observed to be X
Instance 2 of A is observed to be X
Instance 3 of A is observed to be X
Instance 4 of A is observed to be X
Instance 5 of A is observed to be X

(etc.)

Therefore, all A is X

The method of analogy:

A is observed to be X and Y
B is observed to be X and Y
C is observed to be X and Y
D is observed to be X and Y

(etc.)

M is observed to be X and Y
Therefore, M is Y

There are numerous ways to organize and to critique how we process information; any hope of covering them is beyond the scope of this *"Brief" Guide*. However, we need to recognize that elemental structures of thought exist and when we understand them, "we ask important questions implied by these structures."[54] A "Checklist for Reasoning" looks for

1. purpose
2. addresses a question
3. assumptions
4. a point of view
5. data, information and evidence
6. concepts and ideas
7. inferences or interpretations, and
8. implications of research.

We also need to consider intellectual standards as we process information. Variant lists exist, but common among them are those endorsed by the Foundation for Critical Thinking:

1. Clarity
2. Accuracy
3. Precision
4. Relevance
5. Depth
6. Breadth
7. Logic
8. Significance, and
9. Fairness (representing fairly the other viewpoints).

A careful corroboration of evidence helps to ensure these standards in historical studies.

Notes

1. Sometimes the collected evidence takes centuries of review before a reasonable explanation surfaces, such as N. D. Wilson's fascinating explanation about the Shroud of Turin. See "Father Brown Fakes the Shroud," *Books and Culture* (March/April, 2005): 22-29.

2. The Foundation and Center for Critical Thinking provide wonderful resources, including the handy Thinker's Guide Series; see: www.criticalthinking.org. Also see works by John Chaffee, e.g., *Thinking Critically* (New York: Houghton Mifflin Co., 2000) and *The Thinker's Way: Create the Life You Want* (New York: Little Brown and Co., 2000); see www.thinkingworld.com. Also see David Rigg's *A Brief Guide to Virtuous Thinking* and Vern Ludden's *A Brief Guide to Scientific Investigation* (Marion, Indiana: Triangle Publishing, in press).

3. Jerry A. Pattengale, *A History of World Civilizations from a Christian Perspective* (Marion, Ind.: Triangle Publishing); Pattengale, *The Motivated Student: The Dream Needs To Be Stronger than the Struggle* (New York: McGraw-Hill, in press); Pattengale, *Straight Talk: Clear Answers About Today's Christianity* (Marion, Ind.: Triangle Publishing, 2004).

4. For an overview see Pattengale, "Student Success or Student Non-Dissatisfaction" *Growth Journal* (Spring 2006) and Pattengale, "Shoot for the Right Goals" *Chronicle Tribune* (4/17/03, posted at www.indwes.edu/buckcreek).

5. In biblical studies the comparison of manuscripts and ancient versions is important in ascertaining the original text. This corroborative approach is known as "Lower" or textual criticism as opposed to "Higher" or literary criticism. The latter "attempts to determine the questions of the authorship, of the date, and of the composition of any literary text on the basis of vocabulary, style, and consistency." It's somewhat counterintuitive to refer to this as "Higher" criticism, which Edwin Yamauchi credits with the widespread and suspect notion "that the Old Testament is a crazy quilt of unreliable legends . . . " Using this Higher approach, in 1878 Julius Wellhausen launched the "documentary hypothesis" (or JEDP theory) which proposes a late authorship for the Old Testament (ninth to sixth centuries B.C.). This shows strong influence from Darwin and Hegel and gained a large following, but the corroboration of evidence has debunked his views. The above quotes are found in Edwin Yamauchi, *The Stones and the Scriptures: An Introduction to Biblical Archaeology* (Grand Rapids, MI: Baker Book House, 1972): pp. 27-28. This same text also presents a forerunner to the Venn diagram used in this *Brief Guide* to outline corroboration (pp. 158-160). Yamauchi also articulates the key problems with the evolutionary scheme that F. C. Baur (d. 1860) and the Tubingen School apply to the New Testament (pp. 92 ff.). For a more thorough response to the JEDP theory, see Edwin Yamauchi's "The Current State of Old Testament Historiography," in *Faith, Tradition, and History: Old Testament Historiography in Its Near Eastern Context*, A. R. Millard, James K. Hommeier, David W. Baker, eds. (Winona Lake, IN: Eisenbrauns, 1994), pp. 25-36.

6. J. P. Kirsch, "Donation of Constantine," *The Catholic Encyclopedia*, vol. 5 (Robert Appleton Company, 1909); Online edition, 2003, K. Knight.

7. Peter Landesman, "A Crisis of Fakes," *Sunday New York Times Magazine* (03/18/2001): 36.

8. Linda Sillitoe and Allen Roberts, *Salamander: The Story of the Mormon Forgery Murders* (2nd ed., Salt Lake City: Signature Books, 1989); Steven Naifeh and Gregory White Smith, *The Mormon Murders: A True Story of Greed, Forgery, Deceit, and Death* (New York: Weidenfeld & Nicolson Ltd., 1988). See also Roger

D. Launis's review of *Salamander* in the *John Whitmer Historical Association Journal*, 8 (1988): 79-82.

9. Richard Marius, *A Short Guide to Writing about History* (New York: Harper-Collins, 1995): 1. See also: C. Behan McCullagh, *Justifying Historical Descriptions* (Cambridge University Press: New York, 1984), and; Martha Howell and Walter Prevenier, *From Reliable Sources: an Introduction to Historical Methods* (Cornell University Press: Ithaca, 2001).

10. There is evidence throughout history of the lack of historical accuracy. In recent history we know of intentional efforts to misuse noted scholars to rewrite history, such as the case of Hal Lindsey plagiarizing Edwin Yamauchi, and then changing the new text to say the opposite about the ancient Scythians; see Roy Rivenburg, "Question of Attribution," *Los Angeles Times* (Thursday, July 30, 1992): E3.

11. Mary Lynn Rampolla, *A Pocket Guide to Writing in History* (Boston: St. Martin's, 1998): 5.

12. Keith Windschuttle, *The Killing of History: How Literary Critics and Social Theorists are Murdering Our Past* (Australia: Simon and Schuster, 1996; paperback, San Francisco: Encounter Books, 2000), p. x.

13. Hippocrates, *Precepts*, as quoted by Chester W. Starr, *A History of the Modern World*, 3rd ed. (New York: Oxford University Press, 1983), 331. This citation also appears in the helpful book by William Kelleher Storey, *Writing History: A Guide for Students* (New York: Oxford University Press, 1999): 17-18. The original statement by Hippocrates is considerably longer and translations vary widely. For example, in the Loeb Classical Library series (with Greek on the left and the English translation on the right), the sentence in this same quote is translated "For if theorising lays its foundation in clear fact, it is found to exist in the domain of intellect, which itself receives from other sources each of its impressions." He also provides a lively dialogue only garnered from reading more of the original source. In this same section of *Precepts*, Hippocrates states, "But if it begins, not from a clear impression, but from a plausible fiction, it often induces a grievous and troublesome condition. All who so act are lost in a blind alley." See: *Hippocrates*, vol. 1, translated by W. H. S. Jones, Loeb Classical Library Series (Cambridge: Harvard University Press, 1923, 1984), pp. 312-315.

14. James K. A. Smith, *Who's Afraid of Postmodernism?: Taking Derrida, Lyotard, and Foucault to Church* (Grand Rapids, MI: Baker Academic Books, 2006).

15. Robert E. Webber, *Ancient-Future Faith: Rethinking Evangelicalism for a Postmodern World* (Grand Rapids, MI: Baker Books), 1999. Webber looks at the historic responses in the Church to contrary worldviews and finds six paradigms of how it dealt with opposing views.

16. See Arthur F. Holmes, *All Truth Is God's Truth* (Grand Rapids, MI: Wm. B. Eerdman's, 1977). See also Glenn R. Martin, *Prevailing Worldviews of Western Society Since 1500* (Marion, Ind.: Triangle Publishing, 2006). The fulcrum of Martin's text is that the primary question is always theological, i.e., "Is God who He is because of who I am, or am I who I am because of who God is?" He then provides categorical responses to the main philosophical questions. He convincingly argues that anything absolutized apart from God not only defies biblical injunctions, but is illogical given the most tenable answers to the philosophical questions. Martin seems to present a sound use of logic and rationale that defies the trappings James K. A. Smith finds among many of the Modernists; Martin keeps the Lord and his Church central, along with the calling for service. Perhaps Martin would also find value in Robert E. Webber's paradigms and call for a return to the Biblical paradigm. Martin emphasizes a timeless "Biblical Christian Worldview."

17. David Riggs is the Director of the John Wesley Honors College at Indiana Wesleyan University, Marion campus. His forthcoming book is entitled *Divine Patronage in Late Roman and Vandal Africa: Rethinking a Local Narrative of Christianisation* (Oxford University Press). Rodney Stark's argument that Christianity's *rational theology* led to the advancement of Western societies is convincing and should be consulted for serious consideration of the Church and Modernity; see Rodney Stark, *The Victory of Reason: How Christianity Led to Freedom, Capitalism, and Western Success* (New York: Random House, 2005). He argues that within the Western advancements associated with reason, the most important of these victories " . . . occurred within Christianity. While other world religions emphasized mystery and intuition, Christianity alone embraced reason and logic as the primary guide to religious truth" (p. x). Stark's approach to this matter is as candidly confident as K. A. Smith's is cautious. Stark presents a convincing case for the role of rational theology in major scientific, economic and political advances—and this began a millennium prior to the Protestant Reformation. In essence he places reason well within the very paradigm that shook the world and advanced Christianity. His argument also sheds light on the very paradigm Robert E. Webber is calling us to venerate.

18. D. A. Carson, *Becoming Conversant with the Emerging Church*, (Grand Rapids, MI: Zondervan, 2005); also see: "Faith a La Carte?" *Modern Reformation Magazine* (July / August 2005 Issue, Vol. 14.4). In Bob Whitesel's review of my manuscript he noted that the term "Emergent" should likely be kept separate from "Emerging," or at least inform readers of the developments taking place. Emergent is becoming increasingly associated with a select group, almost like a franchising of the Emerging approach. Bob uses "Organic" interchangeably with Emerging. He also notes that in his study of Emerging churches he found them to be solidly based on a rational approach, but it just wasn't as visible in the worship experiences as that found in orthodox churches; see Bob Whitesel, Inside the Organic Church: Learning from 12 Emerging Congregations (Nashville, TN: Abingdon Press, 2006).

19. Webber, *Ancient-Future Faith*, pp. 13-38; see especially charts A-D.

20. "Forgery Bombshell" *Biblical Archaeology Review* (May 16, 2006): http://www.bib-arch.org/bswb00ossuary_Krumbeinsummary.asp.

21. The refreshing aspect of this author's work is that he does not have an ax to grind. He is simply presenting his ideas. Nonetheless, his conclusions (ideas) appear ill-founded.

22. Jules R. Benjamin, *A Student's Guide to History* (New York: St. Martin's Press, 2004), 5.

23. See Ralph Rene's *NASA Mooned America* (1992) and updated articles at http://www.rene-r.com/. Another popular site is Kevin Overstreet's photo analysis challenge of the lunar landings at: http://batesmotel.8m.com/. Although the author of this text finds both of these studies riddled with problems, they're listed for the readers to realize the extent of challenges to common information, and to decide for themselves the validity of such statements.

24. The notions of *The Da Vinci Code* have been thoroughly debunked in numerous texts, and one of the best among the group is Darrell L. Bock's *Breaking the Da Vinci Code: Answers to the Questions Everyone's Asking* (Nashville, TN: Nelson Books, 2004). Also see James L. Garlow and Peter Jones, *Cracking Da Vinci's Code* (New York, NY: Doubleday, 2003).

25. Brock Read, "Can Wikipedia Ever Make the Grade?" *The Chronicle of Higher Education* (October 27, 2006): A31-36.

26. Brock Read, "Co-Founder of Wikipedia, Now a Critic, Starts Spinoff with Academic Editors," *The Chronicle of Higher Education* (October 27, 2006): A35.

27. See Thomas Friedman's *The World Is Flat: A Brief History of the Twenty-first Century* (New York: Farrar, Straus and Giroux, 2005) and his related articles, e.g., "Is Google God or is Friedman an Idiot?" *New York Times* (June 29, 2003).

28. The dean mentioned is Deborah Stipek, Stanford University School of Education, Ibid., p. 54.

29. Claudia Wallis and Sonja Steptoe, "How To Bring Our Schools Out of the 20th Century," *Time* (Dec. 18, 2006): pp. 50-56. The notion of "depth" instead of "breadth" in this *Time* article is the thesis for a different discussion (about the general design of education), but at the core of learning depth is objectivity. See E.D. Hirsch, Jr.'s site, www.coreknowledge.org and his works, e.g., *The Knowledge Deficit* and *Cultural Literacy.*

30. See Irving Hexham, *Encountering New Religious Movements* (Kregel Publications, 2004) and "The Evangelical Response to the New Age," in *Perspectives on the New Age,* edited by James R. Lewis and Gordon Melton (New York, SUNY, 1992), pp. 152-163; also see Kim Riddlebarger, "This Present Paranoia: in *Power Religion: The Selling Out of the Evangelical Church,* J. I. Packer, R. C. Sproul, Allister E. McGrath, Charles Colson, Michael Scott Horton, editor (Chicago: Moody Press, 1992), pp. 278–279.

31. Jasmine Stewart, *The Chronicle of Higher Education*, 39 (June 30, 1993): A28. *Harry Potter and the Sorcerer's Stone* remains a top fiction seller. Its plot is about "A British boy [who] finds his fortune attending a school for witchcraft" (*New York Times Book Review* [August 15, 1999]: 26).

32. We need to remind ourselves that characters like Tolkein's Golum are fictional. His qualities, however, match the pervasive sinister characteristics of villains in real life. The story itself is not true, but the characteristics are true to life and help us in our understanding of truth.

33. Lisa Zunshine, *Why We Read Fiction: Theory of Mind and the Novel* (Columbus, Ohio: The Ohio University Press, 2006), pp. 5, 168.

34. Jerry A. Pattengale, "The Chinese Cultural Revolution Starts a Wave of Repression," *Great Events from History II: Human Rights* (Pasadena: Salem Press, 1992): 1332-1337.

35. This is considered one of the traditional Three Laws of Thought. The other two are The Law of the Excluded Middle *(something either is or is not)* and The Law of Identity *(something is what it is).* As *"fundamental* principles these cannot be shown to be true, since they are the principles by which all *other* claims may be shown to be true." Ed L. Miller, *Questions that Matter: An Invitation to Philosophy* (New York: McGraw-Hill Companies, Inc., 1996), p. 32. Graham Priest, J. C. Beall and Bradley Armour-Garb, editors, *The Law of Non-Contradiction: New Philosophical Essays* (Oxford: Oxford University Press, 2007).

36. Aristotle, *Metaphysics,* 1006a, translated by W. D. Ross in *Basic Works of Aristotle,* Richard McKeon, ed. (New York: Random House, 1941).

37. C. S. Lewis, *Mere Christianity* (San Francisco, CA: Harper Collins, 2001, original copyright, 1952), p. 52.

38. Cf. the museum chart in the back of the Nestle-Aland *Greek New Testament.* The entire Eberhard Nestle Library is housed at The Scriptorium: Center for Christian Antiquities, along with thousands of early manuscripts and printed Bibles. The author co-developed and directed the foundation with Scott Carroll. It was originally located in Grand Haven, MI. The collection is now housed at The Holy Land Experience in Orlando, Florida.

39. See Barbara J. Stevenson, *An Oral History of African Americans in Grant*

County (Charleston, SC: Arcadia Publishing, 2000). Although the text itself is a secondary source it contains numerous primary sources related to the Weaver community. The cover picture was taken on the land just east of our farm where the Weaver school once stood. The building behind the students pictured is the school (we recently found its doors in our barn and restored them—they are now in our entryway). On the bottom right of the cover picture is a young African American boy, around 10 years old. It is Johnny Taylor, discussed in the dedication (pp. iii-iv).

40. Jerry Pattengale, "Reaching a Crossroads Can Teach Us a Lot: There's a History Lesson at Life's every Intersection," Mike Cline, editor, *The Chronicle Tribune* (Gannett Media, 7/13/02). The town of Buck Creek mentioned is around ten miles east of Lafayette, Indiana, and fifty miles west of Weaver.

41. See Nancy E. Botatin et al, *Ramesses the Great: An Exhibition in the City of Memphis* (The City of Memphis, 1987). Also see *24 Hrs. in Cyberspace*. S.v. "Odyssey in Egypt." San Francisco: Against All Odds Productions (February 8-11), 1996 and the centerfold picture in *U.S. News and World Report* (11/21/1996)—the monk is holding my Mac laptop (with its whopping 16 mb memory).

42. Abydos was the cult center of Osiris and contains the memorial temple of Ramesses II (r. 1279-1213 B.C.). W. J. Bankes excavated the site and the list was placed in the British Museum in 1837. Tutankhamen's name is not the only one omitted, as all kings associated with the Amarna heresy are missing, i.e., Akhenaten, Smenkhkare and Ay. See S. Quirke and A. J. Spencer, *The British Museum Book of Ancient Egypt* (London: The British Museum Press, 1992), pp. 30-31.

43. Kevin L. Welch in Jerry Pattengale, *A History,* chapter one.

44. Craig, William Lane, "Did Jesus Rise from the Dead," Michael J. Wilkins and J. P. Moreland, editors, *Jesus Under Fire* (Grand Rapids: Zondervan Publishing, 1995), p. 143.

45. C. Behan McCullagh, *Justifying Historical Descriptions* (Cambridge: Cambridge University Press, 1984), 19, quoted from Craig, "Did Jesus Rise," p. 143. Brackets are mine.

46. The number of research languages was ascertained by his colleagues at Miami University (OH) and announced at his retirement banquet, Shriver Center, Miami University (OH), April 29, 2005 (Oxford, OH); the author was among the speakers and his address, "The Essence of a Mentor," is available upon request. See also the festschrift to Dr. Yamauchi, i.e., John Wineland, editor, *The Light of Discovery: Studies in Honor of Edwin M. Yamauchi* (Eugene, Oregon: Wipf and Stock, 2007).

47. Miller, *Questions that Matter*, pp. 31-54.

48. David Hackett Fischer, *Historians' Fallacies* (San Francisco: Harper & Row, 1970).

49. Ravi Zacharias, The Veritas Forum at Ohio State University (1993), Tape 2, *Tests for Truth—Combinationalism* (Georgia: Ravi Zacharias International Ministries, 1993).

50. A Debate by William Lane Craig and Frank R. Zindler on the subject of "Atheism vs. Christianity: Where Does the Evidence Point?" at the Willow Creek Community Church, Moody Broadcasting Network, June 27, 1993 (312.329.8010).

51. Linda Elder and Richard Paul, Analytic Thinking: How To Take Thinking Apart and What To Look for Why You Do (Foundation for Critical Thinking, 2003), p. 4; also see footnote 2 above.

52. The quoted definitions for deductive and inductive reasoning come from Chaffee, Critical Thinking, pp. 467, 504.

53. Miller, *Questions*, pp. 42-44. The common examples of inductive reasoning are also found in this text.

54. Elder and Paul, *Analytical Thinking*, p. 5; also see "The Logic of History," p. 32.